Sled Dogs in America
The Art of Veryl Goodnight

by Veryl Goodnight and Helen Hegener

Sled Dogs in America:
The Art of Veryl Goodnight

By Veryl Goodnight and Helen Hegener

First printing November, 2024 by Northern Light Media
Book design and layout by Helen Hegener

ISBN 979-8-3304-2842-7

Northern Light Media
1255 South Ridgecrest Road
Wasilla, Alaska 99623-1940

For additional copies of this book visit https://northernlightmedia.org

Cover: *"Under the Spell of Denali"*

This book is dedicated to
Rick and Kate St. Onge
who introduced me to the world of sled dogs
and
To the thousands of dogs
that enabled humans to survive
in the harshest parts of the world.

SLED DOGS WERE TO THE NORTH
WHAT THE HORSE WAS TO THE PLAINS

An artist's creative pursuit is an exciting journey into the unknown. Discovering the many crucial roles sled dogs and their drivers played in history became just such an adventure for me. Once I realized both the time and geographical scope of our partnership with dogs, I began painting with a mission to share their story.

Enjoy the Ride – Veryl Goodnight

My introduction to sled dogs came in 1966 when, as a 15-year-old newcomer to Alaska, I watched Joe Redington Jr. win the Open World Championship Sled Dog Race in Anchorage, and I fell in love with the beautiful huskies who seemed to always be smiling. Several years later, when his father started the 1,049-mile Iditarod Trail Sled Dog Race, I was a volunteer, and huskies have played a large role in my life ever since, culminating in my 2023 book, "The History of Sled Dogs in North America."

Honor the History - Helen Hegener

Detail of "Perseverance"

Sled Dogs in America:
The Art of Veryl Goodnight

Detail of "Unbroken Trail"

"Goodnight understands, and the viewer is also meant to understand, that these beautiful creatures are so much more than pets and loyal companions. They are hard workers with sharp minds and ancient instincts, and their partnership has been crucial to human survival."
—Clover Neiberg in *The Art of the West*, Mar-Apr, 2021

Preface

You ask what it is like to ride a sled.

It is primal.

The dogs are born to run and they love it! They don't just walk off when the snow hook is pulled. They launch and you are initially flying at 18 to 22 mph before they settle into a trot of about 10 mph. While hooking the dogs to the gang line, you cannot hear yourself think from the excited barking. Then it is silent other than the sound of the runners on the snow and the panting of the dogs.

I began mushing at age 60, when most are quitting. My learning curve was steep with one concussion and two black eyes. This entire journey has taught me to appreciate dogs on a far higher level than as a pet. As my husband noted, "Dogs give so much and expect so little." I hope this book will somehow give back to the four-legged companions that have been by the side of humans for thousands of years.

Out of Asia

by Joe May

"Diomede boat crew, Asiatic shore in distance" - Eskimo of Little Diomede Island, by Edward S. Curtis, 1927.

Six millenia before John Steinbeck wrote 'The Grapes of Wrath' with its imagery of the Joad family and all their possessions piled in and on a bastardized Hudson Super Six fleeing the worn-out fields of Oklahoma, bound for California, a 'Promised Land,' an analogous drama played out on the western shores of Bering Strait.

Boethius, an old Roman, said, "History is a wheel." It must be so.

The crude walrus skin boat was dangerously overloaded. Barely a hands-breadth of freeboard showed above the frigid Chukchi waters. The women hadn't been inclined to leave anything behind —choppers, knives, and lamps—all made of stone. The men added to the prodigious load with weapons and tools, more stone, including a skin bag of precious obsidian.

They were going to the New World, reportedly a bounteous land of endless promise, and were determined to arrive prepared for every eventuality—even a shortage of good stone. Asia, the old world in their wake, was history; the new world, the future, loomed on the horizon behind hazy mountain tops, sixty miles away, across the cerulean strait.

Children clambered dangerously over bundles of bedding and skin tents. They hung perilously over the side trailing fingers in the water, and, as children are wont, were impervious to warnings from elders who themselves were awash in adrenalin—giddy with anticipation. Laughter and shouts permeated the air as dogs and puppies dodged between paddlers' feet—barking at swooping sea birds—or just barking for the joy of it. ~•~

Out of Asia

"Chukchi and Eskimo open skin boats were highly seaworthy and could carry many people and goods along stormy coasts or across the Bering Strait for trade, war, and migration. Most new populations migrating from Siberia to Alaska probably arrived in skin boats."

- *The Bark Canoes and Skin Boats of Northern Eurasia* – Smithsonian Books, 2020 – Luukkanen and Fitzhugh

"There is good reason to believe the first human footprints on the American continent were flanked by paw prints."

"Out of Asia" depicts an imaginary family from northeast Asia, migrating across the Chukchi Sea to North America in a walrus-skin boat. The most valuable possessions for survival included their dogs. The idea was inspired by Alaskan legend Joe May, during a visit to his cabin at Trapper Creek, Alaska. He presented me with his essay, along with a challenge to paint the first dogs arriving on the North American continent.

"Out of Asia." 22"H x 44"W, mixed media on paper

Village Kinship

"The known history of sled dogs begins some 10,000 years ago in the Holocene Epoch. Archeological findings on modern Zhokov Island in the East Siberian Sea show that the ice age people of Beringia not only used dogs to draw sleds, they also selectively bred different types of dogs for different jobs, one for hunting and another for mushing." —Thom Swan

Robert Peary's dogs, Nortth Pole, 1910

"Village Kinship." 24"H x 36"W, oil on linen

"Village Kinship." 8"H x 27"W x 10"L, bronze

Dogs were vital to the survival of those who inhabited the North - protecting,
hauling and hunting. Dogs were not considered to be animals, but near human.

Athabascan women with pack dogs in the Copper River Valley, Alaska. Circa 1905.

I was introduced to the freight type of husky in 2014 by Thom Swan of Two Rivers, Alaska. "Swanny" gave me a puppy as part of a program to preserve the traditional Village Dogs that were once the only source of winter transportation in the North. Just as draft horses almost disappeared with the invention of tractors, freight dogs were disappearing in the wake of snow machines. Points Unknown Kennel in Hovland, Minnesota became the main breeding kennel working to preserve historic sled dogs such as my new puppy, Hardy, a Hedlund Husky. I shipped my vintage props to Points Unknown in 2016. Dog handlers wore the clothing I sent and put my leather "collar" harnesses on the dogs. Many works of art were inspired on this trip, including the intimate connection in "Village Kinship." Once home, I worked from life, using Hardy and a young native Yupik neighbor - alternately painting and sculpting mirror images.

Ancient Contract

"There is little doubt that on a long journey, dogs do better on cooked food" — *Hudson Stuck, in 'Ten Thousand Miles with a Dog Sled,' 1914*

Above: Camp on the Valdez Trail, c. 1910

The contract between man and dog was sealed when the first bone was tossed from a cave to a curious wolf pup – we would take care of each other. Winter travelers understood the necessity of caring for their dogs. There are many references of travelers building fires to not only warm themselves and their own food but to provide a warm meal for their dogs.

This wild and natural piece of land near my home has been an ideal setting for many paintings. I built a lean-to from deadfall next to the river to mimic those seen in historical photos and illustrations, as a prop for my own work.

"Dogs seem inextricably bound to humans, their lives interwoven into our lives and our species history."
– excerpt from Mary R. Tahan, *"The Sledge Dogs Who Helped Discover the South Pole"*

"Ancient Contract." 20"H x 32"W, oil on linen

Mail Carriers

Dog teams delivered mail for almost 200 years! The first mail delivered by dog team was in 1778 near Lake Superior, the last was 1963 in Alaska. Mail was delivered as far south as the San Juan Mountains in southwest Colorado. Governments in the northern part of America built shelter cabins along the mail trails. Free to all travelers, the only requirement was to leave wood for the next occupants. More sophisticated "roadhouses" with rooms and dog barns sprang up along the travel routes.

"Winter Refuge." 8"H x 12"W, oil on linen

"U. S. Mail dog team on Yukon River in the winter."
Photographer: P. S. Hunt. circa 1913-1917, Alaska

"The stories, and tales, and the legends about man and dog against the Alaska winter are part of our heritage as Alaskans and Americans. They are truly as great and as important to the story of our country as are the cowboy and Indian stories of the lower 48 states." —Alaska Senator Robert Bartlett, in an address to the U. S. Senate, 1963

"Haven on the Trail." 24"H x 36"W, oil on linen

"News from Home." 15"H x 30"W, oil on linen

Left: U.S. Mail contract driver Comer Cole delivering mail near Kasilof, Alaska. From the Harry T. Becker collection, Alaska State Library [ASL-P67-037b]

Below: Mail bag, U.S. Postal Museum, Washington, D. C.

A mail bag that had supposedly been used in dog team delivery was rolled out for my inspection during a visit to the National Postal Museum in Washington D. C. I subsequently duplicated the bag and made three copies as props for my artwork; however, I was dubious that the bag was authentic. Helen Hegener resolved my doubts when she produced an early 1900's photo of Comer Cole from the Alaska State Library. I used the photo as the foundation for "News From Home." There are, of course, many changes.

When an artist creates a "historical painting," there is often a nagging doubt as to its authenticity. After all, you are viewing the past through the lens of today. We are each a product of our own society and the time in which we live. I breathed a sigh of relief when I saw this photo. It not only verified the mail bags, but the handlebar sled, the type of freight husky the mail carriers depended on, the harnesses the dogs wore, and even the snowshoes leaning on the cabin. What I brought to the painting, from today's social values, is recognition of how deeply dogs respond to human emotions.

The Klondike Gold Rush

On August 17, 1896, the discovery of gold on a tributary of the Klondike River changed the history of the North. A flood tide of humanity would rush to Dawson City. Among the hopefuls was a young man from California named Jack London, a keen observer who noted the splendid dogs who pulled the freight, mail, and passenger sleds. Strong, well-furred dogs were in high demand, sold at a great premium, and a black market soon developed. All along the Pacific coast, from Washington to California, large able-bodied dogs were snatched and transported north to be harnessed and put to work. Jack London immortalized the gold rush dogs in his 1903 novel, *"The Call of the Wild."*

Dogs on a ship in Seattle, bound for the Klondike

Dogs on the trail to Dawson City

$2,000 dog team, Dawson City, Yukon Territory, 1899

On July 17, 1897, the steamship *Portland* docked in Seattle, carrying 68 prospectors and what newspapers immediately termed "a ton of gold." Newspapers quickly spread the word that a great quantity of gold had been found along the remote Thronduick—or Klondike—River in what is today the Yukon Territory, in northwest Canada. What began as a few hundred prospectors sailing north from Seattle soon turned into a stampede of thousands, coming from all over the States. The Klondike Gold Rush had begun, and dogs of every size and kind were suddenly in great demand and sold for high prices, opening a black market in which few dogs were safe from being seized and sold.

Dog team, Dawson City, Yukon Territory, 1899

The Gold Rush Dogs

The vast majority of people living in the lower 48 know very little about sled dogs. However, ask an audience of any age if they read or saw *"The Call of the Wild"* and a sea of hands will pop into the air. "The Gold Rush Dogs" was inspired by Jack London's story of Buck, one of many dogs stolen and sold on the black market during the 1898 Klondike Gold Rush. Desperate men and women would pay $500 to have even one dog to help them haul 1,000's of pounds of supplies to the gold fields. Like London's famous novel, my own work is from the perspective of the dogs.

"The Gold Rush Dogs." preliminary drawing on paper, 20"H x 40"W

Front Street, Dawson City, Yukon Territory, June, 1899

I spent several years collecting photos of dogs that would have been likely candidates for theft. Newfoundlands, St. Bernards, and Great Pyrenees were among those most sought after, as were dogs of the Northland. I sketched many different compositions, trying to find a way to tell their story and finally settled on a still life approach. The Covid shutdown provided an uninterrupted block of time to create "The Gold Rush Dogs."

"The Gold Rush Dogs." Five minute video: https://youtu.be/tUboohl4AZY

"The Gold Rush Dogs." 40"H x 80"W, oil on linen

No Mountain Too High

An older "Sourdough" who knew the country would often partner with someone younger and more physically robust. As few as two dogs give these men an edge. This painting was inspired by the many accounts written in surviving journals, but the image became clear on my own property in southwest Colorado. I enlisted the help of two neighbors - Rick St. Onge on the sled runners and Tyler Willbanks in front. My dogs, Chad and Rosemary, were all too happy to play along. Rosemary spotted a squirrel and everyone followed her upward gaze. The title came in a split second - hope - the singular emotion shared by every prospector from the beginning of time.

"In an era consumed with greed, dogs were sometimes the only ones a lonely gold seeker could trust. They were packhorse, transit system, security guard and pal rolled into one. They were truly worth their weight in gold."

-Claire Murphy and Jane Haigh, *Gold Rush Dogs* (Alaska NW Books, 2001)

"No Mountain Too High." 20"H x 16"W, oil on linen

Reliable Winter Transportation

Dog teams were the only reliable form of winter transportation in snow covered regions into the 1940's. They hauled native hunters and fishermen, early explorers and scientists, miners and missionaries, doctors and lawyers, and many others seeking access to lands beyond the roads and rails.

Thom Swan ("Swanny") of Two Rivers, Alaska, introduced me to historic freight dogs in 2014. These large dogs look nothing like the Siberian Husky most of us picture when we think of "husky," and even less like the small, shorter-coated Alaskan husky that dominates racing today. Freight dogs were a combination of whatever got the job done - malemute, wolf, St. Bernard, Newfoundland, Great Pyrenees and native dogs. These large dogs were also referred to as Village Dogs, or named for the region from which they came. One of my own dogs, Hardy, as well as many of the dogs in my work, are "Hedlund Huskies." As the freight dogs were disappearing in the 1950's, Rose and Nels Hedlund of western Alaska began purchasing some of the best village dogs in order to save the breed. Today the main breeder of these magnificent dogs is Linda Newman, Points Unknown, Hovland, Minnesota. Linda is committed to sharing the thrill of mushing with others. In doing so she is preserving the type of husky that was once vital to life in the North.

"Questioning the Delay." 20"H x 32"W, oil on linen
The wheel dogs were named Nels and Rose, in honor of Nels and Rose Hedlund of Iliamna, Alaska.

"Northwoods Journey." 24"H x 30"W, oil on linen

"Hopeless Tangle." 20"H x 32"W, oil on linen

There is a deep sense of both vulnerability and responsibility when driving a team of dogs. Owning my own team has been a privilege that enabled me to understand and incorporate it into this painting. I shipped historical harnesses and clothing to Points Unknown in Hovland, Minnesota, in January of 2016. Linda Newman's dog handlers drove several teams while she took me ahead on a snowmobile to get photographic reference. When a young dog got off the packed trail and became tangled in the lines, the musher immediately halted the team and went to his aid before he was injured.

"Unbroken Trail." 20"H x 32"W, oil on linen

"In every part of the world the dog is the companion and helper of man, but nowhere is he so essentially part of the life of the people as in the northern part of this continent from Greenland to the Behring Sea."
– Tappan Adney, from *The Klondike Stampede,* 1890

The Denali Suite

March 3, 2019, traveling with fellow artist Ralph Oberg, our plane landed on the frozen expanse of Wonder Lake in Alaska. Denali loomed over us as our guide, Brian Taylor, approached with his team of 13 eager dogs. For the next five days, we enjoyed weather conditions that allowed us to paint on location and photograph working dog teams along this historic route, only 25 miles from the great mountain.

Veryl painting at Denali National Park

Landing on Wonder Lake in Denali National Park, March 3, 2019

"Under the Spell of Denali." 30"H x 48"W, oil on linen

Under the Spell of Denali

In 1913, Harry Karstens and Hudson Stuck were the first to successfully summit 20,310' Denali, North America's highest peak. That ascent, as well as previous attempts, were only possible with the aid of dog teams that carried the supplies over frozen trails. Most climbers today take helicopters to a base camp and use the southern route for their climb. A few intrepid climbers, however, choose the more difficult original route on the north side. To this day, dog teams shuttle their gear across frozen trails and onto the Muldrow Glacier.

Lucky Puppies – Denali Park Canine Patrol
Denali National Park has been patrolled with dog teams since 1922

Each winter, Denali's Park Rangers set out into the wilderness with sled dogs. In doing so they are connecting the past with the present and preserving both the Native and pioneering traditions of Alaska. A litter of puppies is raised annually to replace the retiring 8-year-old dogs. As soon as there is enough snow, the rangers set out with three teams of adult dogs, the puppies running alongside, behind, and sometimes in front. By March they are 8 months old and wearing harnesses for the first time.

| Elsie | Dave Tomeo with Gladys | Benhti | Kusko | Nucha |

My husband Roger and I visited the Denali "School House Litter" in 2021. I make a special effort to paint individual animals rather than generic representations. Shown here as adults, their photos are in the same order as they were when puppies in the painting.

"Lucky Puppies." 30"H x 48"W, oil on linen. Elsie is front on the far left, Gladys is just on the far side of the sled, followed by Benhti. The two boys, Kusko and Nacho, are behind Ranger Julie Carpenter.

"No Time to Spare." 30"H x 48"W, oil on linen

40

The title of this painting refers not only to the incoming storm, but to the rapidly melting snow. Brian Taylor and his powerful dogs haul 1,500 pounds of climbing gear onto the Muldrow Glacier near the base of Denali in advance of the summer climbers. He now has to do this earlier each year, or risk being trapped by a melted ice bridge spanning the raging spring runoff. Cultures that still rely on dogs for winter travel or recreation have had to adapt. The Denali Rangers used to begin their overnight dogsled patrols in late October and could count on winter trails into April. Now they seldom start their patrols until December and often end their dogsled season in mid-to-late March.

Legends of Ashcroft

During World War II, Stuart Mace was assigned to training dogs for Colorado's Tenth Mountain Division. The dog training program was later centralized at Camp Rimini near Helena, Montana. Lt. Mace's Oral History describes training dog teams and their handlers for winter missions that included being parachuted into airplane crash sites. Stuart Mace acquired more than a dozen of "his" huskies when he was discharged in December, 1945. He moved his family to Ashcroft, Colorado, near the now-famous Aspen ski area. He would hook up 13 huskies at the family's Toklat Wilderness Lodge and Husky Kennel and take them into the high country (10,500') of the surrounding Rocky Mountains. Mace always wore an orange scarf made from the canines' parachutes in memory of the many dogs he had trained during the war. Their guests' primal experience of gliding through the magnificent winter landscape behind the powerful dogs ultimately helped the Mace family protect the pristine valley from development.

"Legends of Ashcroft." 26"H x 42"W, oil on linen

Air support in Alaska became critical after the 1941 Japanese invasion of Pearl Harbor. Pilots were hastily trained, and planes were not yet fully capable of handling severe weather. Camp Rimini in Helena, Montana became one of the search and rescue training bases for dogs and men so they could be parachuted into the many resulting plane crash sites. Lt. Stuart Mace was tasked with creating the harnesses and training the dogs which were parachuted into crash locations, where they were met by a dog driver, two surgeons, and a radio man.

The dogs were dropped to precise locations by first using small, bright-colored spotter parachutes. The dog teams expedited getting many injured fliers to help.

Sergeant Preston of the Yukon

The classic 1955-1958 television show "Sergeant Preston of the Yukon" was actually filmed in Ashcroft with the Toklat huskies. Stuart Mace was the trainer and driver of the dog teams for the iconic television series. Richard Simmons played a Canadian Mountie in charge of law and order during the Klondike Gold Rush, assisted by his heroic and faithful husky, Yukon King.

Yukon King

Like many children in the 1950's, I hooked the family dog to my sled and dreamed of owning Sergeant Preston's magnificent husky, Yukon King. As a Colorado native, I realized Stuart Mace had helped shape my own love of the wilderness. It was lingering memories of Sergeant Preston and Yukon King that led me to hook my fearless Jack Russell Terrier to a kick sled as an adult. All of these trails converged to find me with a team of four real sled dogs in my 60's and 70's and at the easel to share the magic of sled dogs.

"Perseverance." 24"H x 30"W, oil on linen

Perseverance

Hardy

I wanted to paint the severe weather conditions described in many harrowing accounts where mushers were saved by their dogs. Colorado gave me ample opportunity to study blizzards in early 2023. I drove out into the worst of the storms, parked in the middle of a road and painted the blizzard that was raging all around me – from the inside of the car. Painting on location is very important to my type of art. Our mind tells us a blizzard is white, but our eyes will tell us differently. The dog team is painted from photos of different dogs collected over years of research. I did not, however, have reference photos of dogs in severe weather. Hardy, my 90-pound freight dog, was more than happy to comply. Facing the painting, Hardy is the wheel-dog (dogs right behind the leaders) on the left.

The Role of Racing

Keeping Alaskan sled dogs from being phased out of existence was one reason why Joe Redington, Sr. started the now famous Iditarod Trail Sled Dog Race in 1973. In 1984, The 1,000-mile Yukon Quest International Sled Dog Race was organized between Fairbanks, Alaska and Whitehorse, Yukon Territory. Joe May's description of the 1986 race in a letter to Veryl—which included his hard-won gold nuggets—illustrates why the Yukon Quest is considered "The World's Toughest Sled Dog Race."

THE 1986 YUKON QUEST INTERNATIONAL SLED DOG RACE

A Testimony to Great Sled Dogs by Joe May

July 2022

Dear Veryl

As promised when this boat project began. Some history:

During the 1986 Yukon Quest, a year the race went in the Fairbanks to Whitehorse direction, a gaggle of teams (13) traveled together from Eagle to Dawson City through a horrendous two day storm of wind, snow, and deadly wind chill. Teams with leaders willing to face the wind took turns leading the caravan until one by one the leaders flat refused to face the blow or bolted away. Straight sections of river, blown completely clear of snow, were polished slick as glass…The blown snow accumulating in the bends and corners into banks a foot to three feet deep and a few yards to hundreds of yards across…Trail markers were long gone on the wind. Constant "gee" "haw" commands to the leaders, already demoralized by wind and glare ice, gradually reduced the number of teams capable of going in front. By dark of the second day only three of us had willing leaders, Jeff King, Sonny Lindner, myself. Through the ground blizzard the lead musher could only see the leaders of the team behind him and often not even his own lead dogs. With darkness it was only a hope that a weak team at the tail end had not failed to keep up, lost contact, and might well perish.

At some point during the night Lindner and I discussed the consequence of attempting to go faster and losing a weak team…or deliberately going slower still with the possible result that none of us would make it. We had no idea how far yet to Dawson. Out of both dog and human food to produce heat and energy, we were all on a knife edge of survival.

Around midnight, during a turn at the front, King's team had had enough…turned away from the wind, and bolted for the bank, to rejoin the column farther back, leaving only Lindner and myself to trade the lead every half hour. The routine was to struggle to each next bend, set the snow hook in an ice crevice, and walk ahead through the drift to break open a trail to the far side…then walk back to the dogs, pull the hook and talk them through the drift quickly before it closed again. At one such turn I came back to the dogs and laid down on the ice beside them to gather strength for another "go." Sonny, waiting behind me, walked up to see why the hold up. He flopped down beside me and we discussed the situation. I remember, I sucked on a frozen stick of pepperoni coated in dog hair and lint that I had discovered at the bottom of a parka pocket. Sonny Lindner is as tough as they come (legend has it he climbed Mt. McKinley without a hat…I believe it.) To paraphrase his words that night, "this is the first time since coming to Alaska that I've been scared. We're lost as lost can be…if we go too fast somebody at the back end could die…if we go too slow we could all die."

We continued on, struggling through the darkness, the wind, and our own uncertainty. Unsure of our location, certain only that we were somewhere on the river, hopeful of not missing Dawson. Sonny and I traded the lead every half hour, cajoling our dogs with every trick we knew, afraid at every bend that they would quit. Sometime in early morning darkness a dim glow materialized through the blow, DAWSON!!!

By chance it was my turn in front and the dogs perked up and searched out a way up the bank to what they knew would be food and rest. Assured we had made it, with a feeling of relief I stopped, set the hook, and walked up to give each dog a scratch on the head and remove a frozen bootie from a wheel dog. Sonny, close behind me, shouted a query as to why the holdup. I yelled back about a frozen bootie and that he should go around me and I'd catch him up at the checkpoint.

I remember his reply still "It was your turn to be in front…only right we should go into town that way, I'll wait," and so that's what we did…his leader's noses right between my runner tails.

The race official/checker emerged from his shelter wearing a welcoming grin. After inquiring as to how many teams we had in tow and their condition he made an announcement: "First team into Dawson this year (something entirely new in the race history) will receive an ounce of gold nuggets and a ton of Eukanuba dog food". I turned to Sonny who could just as well have been first into town but for our turn and turn routine, and who was now standing beside me, gob-smacked by the serendipity of the moment…thousands of dollars lost by his magnanimous gesture of insisting, "after you Joe." Embarrassed, I said something like, "we'll get this right at the finish line"… and we did. I kept the gold and and at the finish banquet signed the dog food receipt over to Sonny. A ton of Eukanuba at the time had more $ value than an ounce of gold.

Afterward, the two day ordeal from Eagle to Dawson became legend and came to be known by the participants as the "86 death march.' We lost no one that night only by the grace of God and four exceptional lead dogs. Five mushers scratched at the checkpoint with severe frostbite, unable to continue, and the rest of us doctored frozen hands and feet during a 24 hour layover that would enable us to tend our dogs and thus finish the race.

While in Dawson I spent 12 glorious hours in Wendy Feller's bathtub (wife of the miner who contributed the gold) with a jug of DMSO for the frozen outer parts and a jug of high proof alcohol for the inner parts… perched handy on the rim of the tub.

These nuggets have moldered on my window sill for 36 years, their only purpose to maintain a bright memory. Now they're your responsibility. Keep the history.

Joe

Keep the History

Antarctica, Greenland, and France

Sled dog team in front of the USMS *North Star in Antarctica, 1939-40*

Not everything that inspires an artist becomes a work of art. In 2010 a litter of nine well-bred Alaskan Huskies was born in Millville, Utah. Professional mushers Rick and Kate St. Onge offered me a puppy. While I was in Utah to get Sasha, Rick loaned me his uncle's diary from the 1939-40 Admiral Byrd Expedition to Antarctica. I was spellbound by the feats the sled dogs were required to perform through deadly weather, over ice and bottomless crevasses. When the expedition was called back due to pending war, Joe Healy smuggled out a puppy, one of the only dogs to return to the mainland. The unjust end to these noble sled dogs was the beginning of my quest to tell their story.

Joe Healy and Antarctica

Joe Healy's Diary

Admiral Richard E. Byrd's U. S. Antarctic Service Expeditions.

Joe Healy was accepted as a dog driver on Byrd's 2nd (1933 – 1934) and 3rd (1939 – 1941) Antarctic Expeditions. His diary and photo album, filled with sled dog pictures, show respect and compassion for dogs in a brutal landscape. One important role of the dog teams was to negotiate the route that Byrd was to fly, laying emergency supply caches in case Byrd's plane went down during his attempt to fly over the South Pole.

On the way to Antarctica

Joseph D. Healy, a member of the United States Antarctic Expedition, halts his sled team for a rest while exploring mountains of the polar region. A cyclometer is attached to the sled to record the distance covered, an important instrument for polar travel. June 7, 1941.

World War II – Greenland to Paris

Healy returned to the U.S. from Antarctica in May, 1941 with a single husky puppy he named Rinsky hidden under his coat. He then joined the Army Air Corps, serving in Greenland, conducting search and rescue missions under the command of Lt. Bernt Bachen. Healy's now grown husky, Rinsky, played a major role in extraordinary rescues. After Greenland, Sgt. Healy was called on for another war effort. He accompanied 200 sled dogs to the front of the battle in Europe. Dog teams were intended to serve as ambulances, but circumstances prevented the dogs from serving in WWII.

"Early in the spring of 1943, Rinsky led a crack dog team across Greenland's bleak ice cap in a successful rescue of the crew of a plane that had crashed five months before. Bypassing dangerous crevasses and plowing over vast furrowed snowfields on the windswept ice cap, Healy and his dogs saved several lives." —*YANK: the Army Weekly*, January 14, 1944

Joe Healy and his lead dog Rinsky in Greenland, June 1, 1942

The 1925 Serum Run: The Great Race of Mercy

In the winter of 1925, the remote gold rush town of Nome was threatened by a diphtheria epidemic. In one of the coldest winters on record, twenty of the best mushers in Alaska, most of whom were native Athabaskan U.S. mail carriers, were organized to relay antitoxin serum 674 miles from the train depot in Nenana to Nome. Newspapers reported their progress daily and the world watched in awe as the brave mushers and their dog teams made their way north and west to the stricken town in just over five days.

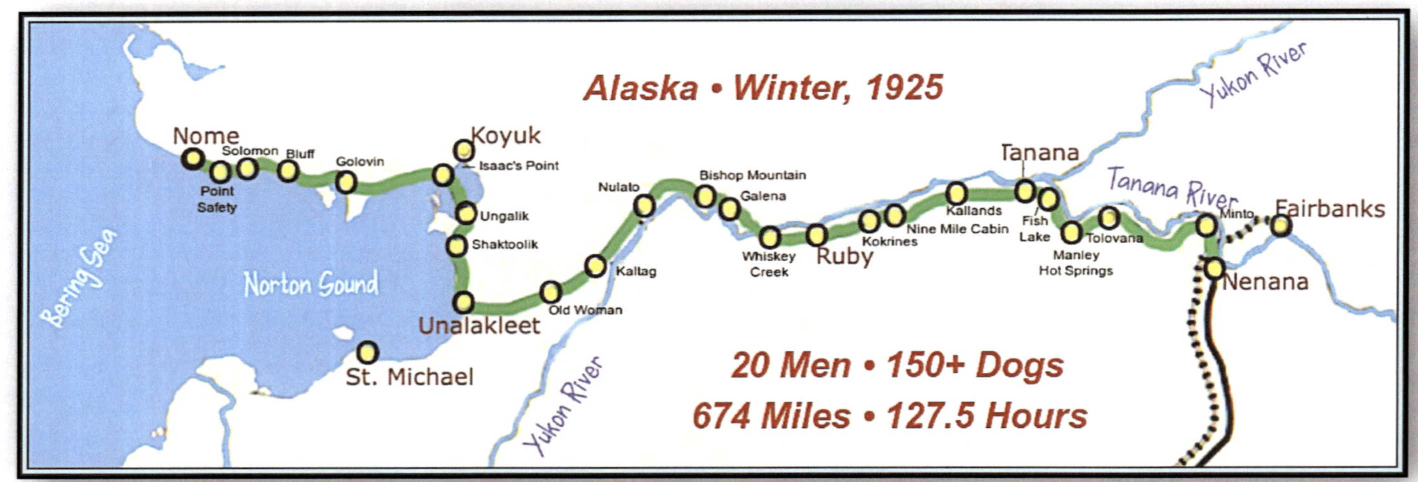

"Science made the antitoxin that is in Nome today, but science could not get it there. All the mechanical transportation marvels of modern times faltered in the presence of the elements… Other engines might freeze and choke, but that oldest of all motors, the heart, whose fuel is blood and whose spark is courage, never stalls but once." ~*The New York Sun*, February, 1925

Meanwhile racing legend Leonhard Seppala and his dog team, led by twelve-year old Togo, were sent from Nome to intercept the serum. Racing toward the oncoming mushers, Seppala took a shortcut across the ice of Norton Sound. By sheer good luck, musher Henry Ivanhoff, now in possession of the serum, had just departed Shaktoolik on the shore of Norton Sound and was able to hail down Seppala and hand off the serum. Seppala turned the tired team around, and Togo once again led them back across the treacherous open ice of Norton Sound. They had traveled 91 miles in one day.

Gunnar Kaasen was a dog driver who worked with Seppala, hauling freight for a Nome mining company. When called on to assemble a team and join the relay drivers, Kaasen chose a large black dog he had admired named Balto to lead along with a proven leader, Fox. They successfully took possession of the precious serum and began the return trip to Nome through a blizzard so severe, Kaasen could not see his dogs. Balto and Fox were on their own to find the trail – and they did it – arriving in Nome at 6 a.m. on February 2, 1925.

The Exhibit

Western Spirit Museum of the West
A Smithsonian Subsidiary
Scottsdale, Arizona
presents
Veryl Goodnight and Helen Hegener
Honoring the extraordinary contributions
of sled dogs and their drivers
to the history of our country

The concept of sled dogs being exhibited in the desert is not as unlikely as it seems. The Navajos and the Apaches are part of the Athabascan speaking peoples. It is believed that the Athabascans originated in Asia and crossed the Bering Strait during the previous Ice Age. These first immigrants to North America almost certainly traveled with their dogs as one of the most important tools for survival in the harsh North.

The sled dog has bookended the history of modern humans in North America from the first crossings over the land bridge—or in skin boats across the sea—to winter patrols in Denali National Park today.

Western Spirit Museum embraced Veryl's vision of sharing the largely untold stories of sled dogs and their drivers. With the generous assistance of Alaskan historian Helen Hegener, the sled dog is finally being recognized for many of the roles they have been asked to fill in the service of man.

Michael Clawson, the Executive Editor for *Western Art Collector*, previewed "Sled Dogs in America - Alaska and Beyond" in the July 2024 issue:

"'Horses of the North' places the untold stories of sled dogs in the center of the Western Art world."

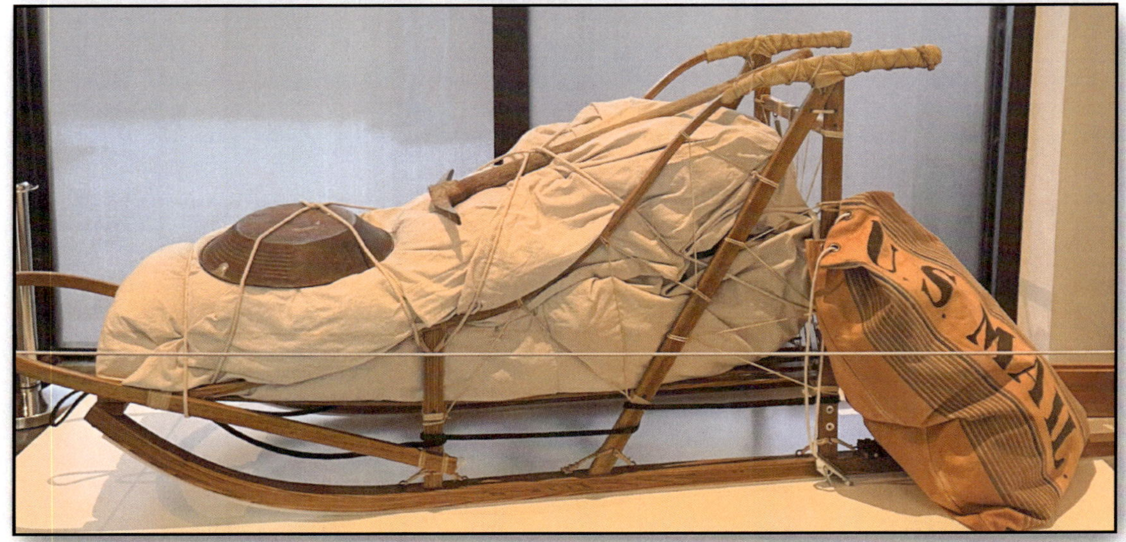

Artist Props

Replica of early 1900's wheelbarrow-handled dog sled
Replica of U.S. Postal mail bag used for dog team mail delivery
Original miner's pick and pan

World War II parachute
and sled dog harness
On loan from the
Collection of Lynn Mace

The original letter from legendary Alaskan musher Joe May to Veryl relates, in detail, the severe weather during the 1986 Yukon Quest International Sled Dog Race (see pages 50-51). Joe was awarded an ounce of gold nuggets for being the first into Dawson City. He gave the gold to Veryl for tackling the challenge of painting the first dogs to arrive in North America by crossing the Chukchi Sea ("Out of Asia," see pages 10 and 11).

The letter is signed
"Keep the History."

**Wtih Great Appreciation to Western Spirit Museum
for enabling me to honor Joe's request.
Veryl**

Veryl Goodnight

Veryl Goodnight has dedicated her life to exploring the relationships between humans and animals through bronze sculptures and oil paintings. As a wildlife rehabilitator, horse owner, and dog lover, Goodnight shares her life with animals that often become models. Veryl's extensive body of work includes over 200 unique sculptures, 20 monuments and countless paintings. Her award-winning art has been displayed throughout the country at museums, zoos, universities, presidential libraries, and in places as far-reaching as Berlin to Beijing and Botswana.

A large format hardcover book titled *"No Turning Back – The Art of Veryl Goodnight,"* was published in 2011 to correspond with a forty-year retrospective at the Gilcrease Museum in Tulsa, Oklahoma. She was inducted into the National Cowgirl Hall of Fame in 2016 for a lifetime of representing the American West in her art. Her best known monument, *"The Day the Wall Came Down,"* is a larger-than-life bronze depicting five horses leaping over the crumbled Berlin Wall. There are two "sister castings" of this 7-ton monument - one outside the Allied Museum in Berlin, Germany and one at the Presidential Library in College Station, Texas.

A Colorado native, Veryl's career started as a wildlife painter in the early 1970's. She began sculpting to educate herself about anatomy. Sculpture then dominated her career throughout the late 1900's while she and her husband, Roger Brooks, lived in Santa Fe, New Mexico. Their 2006 move back to Colorado fulfilled a lifetime desire to live in the mountains. Their property is situated between 11,900' Helmet Peak and Mesa Verde National Park. The Middle Mancos River, complete with intermittent resident beaver, creates a natural wildlife preserve and constant inspiration.

The spectacular surroundings expedited Veryl's return to oil painting. Sled Dog races in the surrounding San Juan National Forest opened a new chapter in Veryl Goodnight's five decades long career.

Original Paintings
Limited-Edition Giclees
Bronze Sculptures
Available at www.verylgoodnight.com
Contact: veryl@verylgoodnight.com

"The Day the Wall Came Down."
Seven-Ton Monument to Freedom
Allied Museum - Berlin, Germany
and the George H. W. Bush Presidential Library, College Station, Texas

"Morning Jingle."
32"H x 60"W oil on linen
Collection of the A Bar A Ranch
Encampment, Wyoming

"A New Beginning." Life-sized Bronze, Edition 15. Two public locations: Downtown Cheyenne, Wyoming and History Colorado - Denver, Colorado

"Golden Plains of Yesteryear."
30"H x 48"W oil on linen
Collection of the Artist

"No Bed of Roses."
24"H x 40"W oil on linen
Collection of Desert Caballeros Museum - Wickenburg, Arizona

RESOURCES for the ADVENTURER

SO YOU WANT TO TRY IT?
There are many outfitters world wide that offer
sled dog rides and multi-day tours.
Below are the two outfitters that helped me.

POINTS UNKNOWN - Dog Sledding and Wilderness Adventures
Owner and Breeder of Hedlund Huskies - Linda Newman
Note: Art inspired at Points Unknown include *Village Kinship*,
Hopeless Tangle and *Northwoods Journey*
Located on the North Shore of Lake Superior
82 Irish Creek Road • P. O. Box 51
Hovland, MN 55606
218-370-0283
linda@points-unknown.com
Website: www.points-unknown.com

MOON DOG KENNEL
Owners: Brian Taylor and Courtney Green
Note: Brian and his dogs are the models in *No Time to Spare*.
Authentic Alaskan Experiences Year Round
Hiking across the tundra with puppies
or mushing to a remote cabin.
Located North of the Denali Park Entrance
Mile 3.5 Stampede Road, Healy, Alaska
907-987-5060
moondogkennelak@gmail.com
www.moondogkennel.com

RESOURCES for the ARMCHAIR MUSHER

There are hundreds of exciting books to take your imagination down snow laden trails.

The History of Sled Dogs in North America, by Helen Hegener
Alaskan Sled Dog Tales, by Helen Hegener
Ten Thousand Miles with a Dog Sled, by Hudson Stuck
Dog-Puncher on the Yukon, by Arthur Treadwell Walden
Baldy of Nome, by Esther Birdsall Darling
The Cruelest Miles: The Heroic Story of Dogs and Men in a Race Against an Epidemic, by Gay & Laney Salisbury
On Time Delivery: The Dog Team Mail Carriers, by William S. Schneider
Racing Alaskan Sled Dogs, by Bill Vaudrin
The Klondike Stampede of 1897-1898, by Tappan Adney
Soldiers and Sled Dogs: A History of Military Dog Mushing, by Charles L. Dean
The Sledge Patrol: A WWII Epic of Escape, Survival and Victory, by David Howarth
Harnessed to the Pole: Sledge Dogs In Service to American Explorers of the Arctic, 1853-1909, by Sheila Nickerson
Frozen in Time: A Story of Survival and a Modern Quest for Lost Heroes of WWII, by Mitchell Zuckoff
and - of course
Call of the Wild, by Jack London

Gratitude

Rick and Kate St. Onge
Introduction to sled dogs, mentoring my learning curve on the runners
Bringing Sasha, Chad and Rosemary into my life and work -
Rick, for being the perfect model in five paintings.

Thom Swan, "Swanny"
Historical advice, introduction to Freight Dogs, modeling and the priceless gift of "Hardy"

Joe May
Words that inspired

Linda Newman
Preserving the Hedund Husky

Ralph Oberg
Sharing artistic inspiration and enabling the trip into Denali National Park

Brian Taylor
Guiding in Denali National Park

The Denali Canine Park Patrol
Complete cooperation in sharing the unique history

Lynne Mace
Sharing family history of Stuart Mace

Bob, Joe and Kate St. Onge
Sharing the family history of Joe Healy

Christine Mollring
Representing my work since the 1970's

Henry Terry
Western Spirit Museum Exhibit Designer

Charlie and Jennifer Sands
Generous Sponsors of "Sled Dogs In America - Alaska and Beyond"

Roger Brooks – Unfailing Love and Support

Helen Hegener
Tireless research to ensure historical accuracy in the exhibit, this book,
and for including my work in her magnificent volume
The History of Sled Dogs in North America

Western Spirit – Scottsdale's Museum of the West
For sharing the largely unknown history
Sled Dogs In America – Alaska and Beyond

DOGS GIVE SO MUCH AND
EXPECT SO LITTLE